USING HOUSES AND HOMES

Stephen Allen
Liz Hollinshead
Sue Wilkinson

ENGLISH HERITAGE

CONTENTS

Nightingale Tower, Woolwich.

Peter Holinshead

ABOUT THIS BOOK

A country cottage with wisteria and roses growing up the walls, an historic house with acres of gardens, a suburban semi-detached, a medieval castle, a high rise flat: all of these dwellings are different, but all of them have many things in common as well. All provide for basic needs such as shelter and warmth, but they all do so in different ways.

Houses are social and historical resources. Many houses have had long and varied lives; they reflect changes in social patterns and stand as evidence of people and their environment both past and present.

The way a home is defended, constructed, furnished and decorated tells us about the people who lived in it.

Teaching and learning from houses and homes allows pupils to work with physical evidence and to develop a variety of skills and concepts. Every part of the History National Curriculum at all Key Stages has a focus on domestic life, and a study of the development of houses leads into exploration of vital cross-curricular themes of Economic and Industrial Awareness, Citizenship and Environmental Studies.

This book looks at how houses have developed and changed through the ages and at how pupils can use them to explore both the fabric of the buildings and the lives of the people who lived in them. There are suggestions for strategies and activities for work both on site and in the classroom, and ways in which other subject areas can be integrated into the topic are investigated.

Lastly, houses are an accessible resource. A wide range of houses, both old and contemporary, will be found within easy travelling distance of most schools.

HISTORY OF HOUSING

Very few of us live in historic houses or even houses that are more than 100 years old. Nevertheless, the houses we live in have their own histories. This chapter looks at the history of housing and how the buildings we live in have developed.

EARLY HOUSES

The first houses in Britain were built over 7000 years ago by people who gathered wild foods and hunted. These Mesolithic people built small, circular houses with walls made from wooden stakes. Traces of the houses of the first farmers between 4000 and 3000 BC show that they were big, rectangular buildings or halls, made from large timbers. The doorway was often at one of the corners and some of the houses were partitioned inside.

The houses of the Late Neolithic and Early Bronze Age (3000 to 1500 BC) were small and round or oval with a central fireplace. In the Later Bronze Age (1500-900 BC) houses were round and much larger, with floor areas often over 100 sq m – larger than the ground floor areas of our own homes today. Extended families of 20 to 30 people could have lived comfortably in them. From this period onwards, houses were built with deep, firm foundations. The conical roof was held up by large wooden posts and the walls were constructed of wattle and daub – branches woven between the posts and plastered with a mixture of mud, straw and dung. The doorway faced south, the best direction for sunlight and protection from the wind. These roundhouses were often grouped into an enclosure and were surrounded by fields divided by ditches and trackways.

From the Late Bronze Age into the Iron Age (900 BC – AD 43) there were changes in the way that people lived. Large communities of 40 or more households might live

Late Bronze Age to Early Iron Age roundhouses at Danebury Hillfort, Hampshire. Artist's impression by Karen Guffogg.

Inside the dining room at Lullingstone. Artist's impression by Peter Dunn.

within hillforts such as Danebury, surrounded by large earthwork defences. Also the entrances of most Iron Age round houses now faced towards the midwinter and equinox sunrise. Indoor activities were probably organised according to the movement of the sun: people

worked in the southern side of the house, where they cooked, ground corn, weaved and made pottery, and slept on the north side.

During the Roman occupation, many people continued to live in round houses but new styles of living were adopted, initially by

Outside and inside an Anglo-Saxon house.

The keep, Orford Castle, Suffolk.

local aristocrats. Towns were carefully planned with impressive civic buildings, rectangular street patterns, shops and private houses. Many urban houses had several rooms and at least two storeys, being solidly built out of stone, brick, tiles, concrete and wood. Wood framing was used for the

Inside the great hall of Orford Castle, Suffolk. Artist's impression by Alan Sorrell.

Lullingstone Roman Villa, Kent. Artist's impression by Graham Sumner.

upper floors. In the countryside the wealthy families built villas within their rural estates. These large multi-roomed buildings were richly decorated with mosaic floors and painted plaster walls and contained under-floor heating systems and bath houses. The ordinary people lived in single storey rectangular houses built largely of wood but often with stone footings.

After the departure of the Roman army and administration and the arrival of the Saxons and other settlers from across the North Sea, people shunned the towns and the villas. No houses were built of stone and the rectangular wooden farmhouses incorporated both Saxon and local building styles. The wooden framed houses were up to 9 m long and 5m wide, with a central hearth, wattle and daub walls without windows and a thatched or turf-covered roof. Buildings were organised into compounds comprised of a main farmhouse and a series of outhouses such as the small sunken-floored sheds which were often used for weaving. Although livestock were occasionally kept in one end of the farmhouse, as was the practice in the Saxon homelands, this was probably rarely done in Britain.

THE MEDIEVAL PERIOD

The houses which survive from the medieval period are not just the homes of the rich and powerful, but include many smaller homes in both towns and rural areas. Castles were built in order to establish Norman control over the surrounding area, but they also combined

The great hall at the medieval manor house of Stokesay Castle, Shropshire.

domestic accommodation within the military headquarters. Initially, the lord's family lived within the keep, but as peace became more established, they moved to more comfortable quarters within the bailey.

Medieval manorial houses, as well as being homes, were also the centre of the local feudal economy. Some incorporated defensive features: such houses were usually stone-built, but timber-framed houses, often belonging to farmers and merchants, have also survived.

The principal part of a medieval house was an open hall with a large hearth, where everyone met and ate together. The outlet for the smoke was simply a hole or louvre in the roof; fireplaces were added later. Kitchens were often placed outside

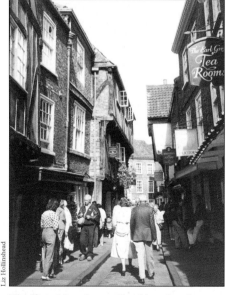

The Shambles, the medieval butchers' street, in York. Some of the original medieval houses have been replaced but continue to be built on the same plots, perpetuating the narrow, cramped street line.

the main building in order to minimise the fire risk.

The medieval period saw a gradual move towards greater privacy with separate rooms developing for different functions. In manor houses the hall remained a communal room but separate sleeping and living chambers were established for the lord's family and the more important guests. This apartment was known as the solar, and traditionally was situated at the opposite end of the hall from the kitchen and service rooms. Houses also became more comfortable. Those who could afford it plastered and painted their walls or covered them with woven hangings; glazed their windows and built indoor lavatories, called garderobes. Many of these comforts were portable; people of high rank travelled with their households from one property to the next, taking their wall coverings and even their glass windows with them.

The medieval house often combined a work and storage area with private living accommodation. In town houses the close mixture of commercial and residential use caused many hazards. Regulations were introduced in many towns to improve public health, protect privacy, prevent encroachment of properties and guard against fire.

The houses of the very poor do not survive, as they were built of materials that were cheap and plentiful, which are generally those which decay easily. Richard Carew, writing in the 1580s, described the house of a poor person as being "walls of earth, low thatched roofs, few partitions, no glass windows".

THE GREAT ENGLISH HOUSING REVOLUTION

In the sixteenth century the growing wealth of the merchants, and what we would call the middle classes, and the availability of new building materials and techniques, created new expectations of comfort. This brought about what has been described as the English Housing Revolution, or the Great Rebuilding. The concern was less

Classical details at the late sixteenth-century Kirby Hall, Northamptonshire.

THE AGE OF THE GREAT HOUSE

By the end of the sixteenth century defence was not a priority for the very rich, but a display of wealth and style was. Renaissance styles from France, Italy and Germany influenced the design of grand houses which began to incorporate classical detailing both in the exterior and interior decoration. Large regular windows, towers and high chimneys added to the feeling of grandeur. Many medieval halls were renovated and modified, and the new fashions were copied in the design of smaller houses.

The seventeenth and eighteenth centuries brought more changes to the way houses of the rich looked. Great emphasis was placed on symmetry, formed by regular shapes and the use of pillars, and on grandness which was expressed in the magnificent entrances, large windows and impressive staircases. This was done on a large scale, as well as in smaller town houses found in many London squares and in spa towns like eighteenth-century Bath.

Classical influence continued to dominate more modest town houses until the Victorian period. These are in Hackney, London.

with security and more with privacy and opulence: houses began to be built more commonly of stone and of the new, prestigious material, brick. Walls were wainscotted; glass windows became more common; fireplaces, with chimneys to take away smoke and soot replaced the open hearth.

In towns such houses existed side by side with the dwellings of the poor. The cramped conditions and the prevalence of wooden structures meant that fire was a constant hazard and countless properties were destroyed. In the seventeenth century the government and many local authorities, like Great Yarmouth, tried to force builders in towns to use only brick and stone, but these regulations were irregularly enforced and often ignored in many places.

Fairfax House, York, a town house with the classical influence of symmetry, pillars and pediments.

Victorian town house in Northampton.

Parnell House, Streatham Street, London, one of the
properties provided for the poor by Charles Peabody.

Houses in the model village of Saltaire, Bradford, built for his workers by Titus Salt. The large house on the corner is for an overseer,
whilst the rest were for the ordinary workers.

THE SPREAD OF TOWNS

The eighteenth and nineteenth centuries also saw the planning of town housing as builders and architects built housing for the upper and middle classes. As towns moved out of their medieval boundaries, so the rich sought healthier environments in which to live. The villas of the middle classes were built on the outskirts of towns because improved transport links enabled people to live out in the outlying areas whilst working in the centre. The housing of the rich in the suburban areas became increasingly separate from that of the poorer city dwellers.

The growth of towns and cities during the Industrial Revolution brought a huge growth in the urban population. New technology, the mass production of brick, and cheap labour made possible the building of the large number of houses needed. Many were built to standard designs such as the back-to-back houses and shared privies of the poor, and the two-parlour and terraced houses with outside lavatories of the artisan. These designs were copied from town to town. Larger town houses, often in terraces, were also built to house the middle and upper class families and their servants.

The growth of cheap "slum"

housing and the overcrowding of cities caused outbreaks of cholera and typhoid. Sanitation inside the house was possible only for those who could afford it. As these problems worsened so both local and national government enforced housing and health regulations and standards.

Philanthropists, appalled by the slums of the industrial towns, looked to provide a model for housing the working classes. Charitable trusts were established such as the Peabody Trust, set up in 1862 by an American, George Peabody, who aimed to "ameliorate the conditions and augment the comforts of the poor". Octavia Hill purchased slums and 'reformed' the tenants by tight control and management, mixing low rent and self improvement to change "a mob of semi-paupers into a body of self-dependant workers". The garden city movement, begun by Ebenezer Howard who built Letchworth Garden City in 1904, aimed to give each house its own space and distinctive style. These ideas were taken up in the design of many later housing developments.

BOOM YEARS FOR HOUSE BUILDING

Lloyd George's promise to build homes fit for heroes at the end of the First World War introduced a rapid programme of house building as the government subsidised the construction of both council and private houses. The idea of owning one's own dream home in suburbia away from the dirt of the city captured the popular imagination. Row upon row of neat terraces, and avenues of tidy semi-detached houses became a feature of towns and cities. These houses were built to appeal to the owners' tastes and aspirations, with small gardens, and decorative features added to roofs and windows.

The Second World War also had a great impact on housing. German bombs had cleared many of the city slums and governments struggled to meet the housing needs of the population. The answer was to

1930s middle class surburban terrace housing, Southwark, London.

Commuters were encouraged to move out of London to housing adjoining railway links. This is the cover of the Metropolitan line's Metro-land booklet of 1920 featuring the ideal suburban home.

provide high-density dwellings, architects often preferring to build up rather than out. Many homes were built as flats, low and high rise, using concrete and with flat roofs and overhead walkways. In order to keep down the costs of house building the standards of materials and construction were often lowered. Many of these high rise flats, once seen as the solution to housing needs, are now being pulled down to make way for smaller developments.

More recently new town developments have moved back to the use of brick and slate in their construction, and to the idea of each house having its own space or garden. The latest technology is

Flats with walkways and connecting bridges, Park Hall Estate, Sheffield.

used to provide every comfort and convenience in the design of new houses, some of which are built in copies of traditional styles, and in older houses, which are renovated to suit current tastes.

Vernacular houses

These are houses of small to medium size built in local materials and styles, using the skills of individual masons and carpenters. In the many areas where stone was not readily available, timber was used as a frame and the intervening space was filled in with whatever material was available, tiles, cob, bricks, or most commonly, wattle and daub. Owing to advances in manufacturing techniques and transport facilities in the nineteenth century, bricks became cheap and plentiful and largely replaced local materials.

Cob, a clay and straw mixture, was used in the south west. This house has been renovated using traditional methods.

Timber-framed cottage from Cheshire.

Distinctive tiles are used as a covering in south eastern counties. This one is from Horsham, Sussex.

ASKING THE RIGHT QUESTIONS

By looking closely at a building and asking relevant questions, pupils can find out about it for themselves. There are five types of questions which can be used as a framework in examining the evidence. They are:

■ WHAT questions: what is this place for – what needs was this house designed to meet?

■ HOW questions: how was it built?

■ WHY questions: why was it built? why was it built here?

■ WHEN questions: when was it built? when was it changed?

■ WHO questions: who built it? who lived here?

What and how questions make a good starting point for any work on site. They require pupils to think about a house as a system, as a place people lived in and as a building designed to meet certain needs. Once the what and how questions have been investigated there will be lots of information to help in working out the who, when and why.

WHAT NEEDS IS A HOUSE DESIGNED TO MEET?

Pupils need to think first of all about what houses can provide. A good way to introduce this is to ask them to look at their own homes first. In a class of thirty, all living in different types of dwellings, they will find that all their homes have certain things in common; they have all been designed to meet certain basic needs. These are:

■ shelter

■ security

■ lighting

■ warmth and cooking

■ water supply and sanitation

Once pupils have established what houses are designed to do they can apply this to any site they visit by looking at the way that these particular needs have been met.

Shelter

This is the most basic function of a dwelling and is provided by the roof and walls, which protect against sun, wind and rain. When rains hits the roof, it has to be deflected elsewhere, otherwise the accumulated water brings the whole structure down. Most roofs are angled to shed water, which is then directed downwards, avoiding the walls. At the base of the roof the water runs straight off or is is collected in gutters and directed downward through pipes. Flat roofs have a gutter system and either drainpipes or protruding overflow pipes. Drain pipes were originally

Walls are not always in one vertical plane. Alexandra Road Estate, London.

English Heritage Photo Library

made of wood or lead, and were only used on the houses of the well-off, but mass production of cast iron, and later, of plastic, has made them the norm on most houses.

On site pupils can examine the shape of the roof, and work out how efficiently the water is directed downwards. Do the eaves overhang so that the walls are avoided? In houses that are not rectangular, what is the shape of the roof? Does this cause problems with directing the water away? How are the exposed ends of the roofing material finished off?

Walls need to be windproof, waterproof and continuous, except for a point of access. Walls are generally a flat perpendicular plane, but not always. Round structures are stronger than ones with squared corners, and were used in defensive buildings. In the 1930s there was a trend to add rounded corners and details, and some modern flats rise

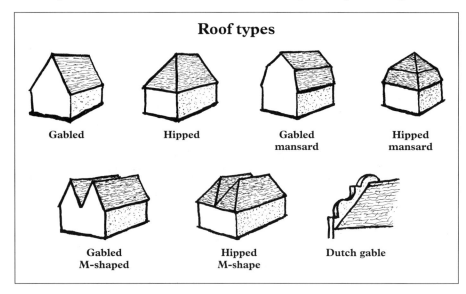

Roof types

Gabled

Hipped

Gabled mansard

Hipped mansard

Gabled M-shaped

Hipped M-shape

Dutch gable

in receding balconied steps. Ask pupils why the walls of the building they are studying are the shape they are – is it for strength, convenience, defence, fashion, conformity to a street pattern, or a building converted from another use?

Entrances have changed according to availability of different materials, manufacturing techniques, fashion and the security needs of the day. They carry lots of clues which pupils can pick up about the owner's taste, status, and the technology of the times as it is displayed in the materials used, for example in the lock, hinges, handle, bell or knocker, and other door furniture.

Security

The basic aims of security are to keep the unwanted out, and to protect the property and its occupants. For some people security is also linked to privacy; they want to be free from prying eyes. The methods people use today to protect their homes are very different from those used in the past. From a study of their own and other people's home pupils will have a number of ideas about the way we keep houses secure today:

■ reinforced doors and windows locks, chains, bolts

■ burglar alarms (even fake ones)

■ external lighting

■ electronic devices

■ net curtains

■ timer switches on the lights so that they come on when people are out

■ beware of the dog signs

■ external fences/railings

■ neighbourhood watch stickers in the window

■ hedges

■ gates with locks on them or electronic gates

■ entry phones

■ porters on duty to control entry to a building.

Queen's entrance, Audley End, Essex, early seventeenth century.   **Georgian door with fanlight.**   **Victorian town house door.**   **Rennie MacIntosh terraced house door, early twentieth century.**

Liz Hollinshead/W John Brown

How is the door fixed?

In very early houses entrances were most probably closed with hurdles or leather curtains. The first doors had no special framework to fit against and were made from heavy planks battened together. They were fixed into the wall or floor by protruding pivots, but this form of hinge was replaced by wrought iron flat hinges, which hooked over hangers in the wall. The introduction of door frames cut down on draughts, and the introduction of lighter wood, like pine, resulted in doors which were much lighter. This meant that hinges could become much less substantial, and the H design hinge was developed. By the end of the seventeenth century sophisticated carpentry techniques promoted the production of very lightweight doors with decorative panels, and this, together with the desire for symmetry led to the introduction of the concealed butt hinge.

Security at a medieval manor house

Stokesay Castle in Shropshire is a manor house which was fortified in the thirteenth century to protect it against Welsh raiders.

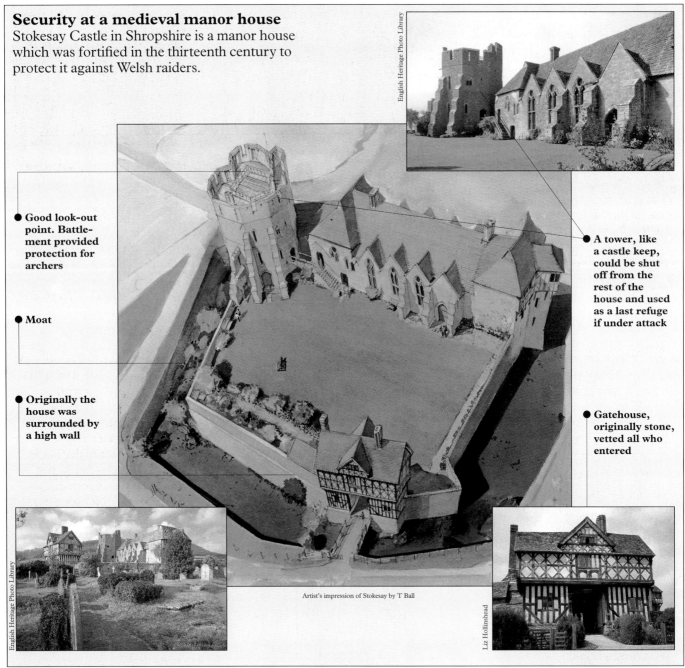

● **Good look-out point. Battlement provided protection for archers**

● **Moat**

● **Originally the house was surrounded by a high wall**

● **A tower, like a castle keep, could be shut off from the rest of the house and used as a last refuge if under attack**

● **Gatehouse, originally stone, vetted all who entered**

Artist's impression of Stokesay by T Ball

Your class can compare this list with the range of options open to people in the past. As now, windows and doors were the most likely points of entry for unwanted visitors. Doors had locks, bolts or draw bars, and vulnerable windows could be barred or shuttered. At one extreme, castles, the homes of the powerful, were built with defence as a priority. Keeps had thick walls, a first floor entry which left attackers exposed on the external stairs, no ground floor windows, stout doors with defences like a drawbridge, portcullis and murder holes; towers to give defenders a good view and unimpeded aim at those below, battlements to hide behind, and all surrounded by a curtain wall and ditch or moat. Early medieval houses had living accommodation on the first floor, with small ground floor windows and access only by external stairs. Others, including monasteries and great country houses had gatehouses or lodges set within boundary walls. In later town houses, front doors were kept locked, and entry at the back led straight into busy service areas where intruders would be immediately noticed. Poorer houses were often left unlocked, the few valuables being hidden or locked away.

Shuttered window.

Holes for security bars.

Panes of glass set at different angles to catch maximum light throughout the day. Sixteenth-century stone mullioned window, Haddon Hall, Derbyshire.

Carved, wooden sixteenth century frames.

Georgian sash windows.

Early Victorian decorative window.

1930s coloured glass 'sunburst' window.

Windows

1950s window.

Window size reflects the status of the room behind

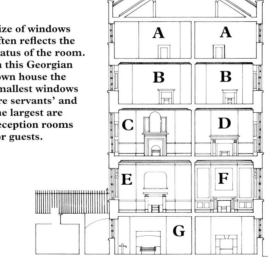

Size of windows often reflects the status of the room. In this Georgian town house the smallest windows are servants' and the largest are reception rooms for guests.

Top floor	A: servants' bedrooms or nursery
Second floor	B: family bedrooms
First floor	C: drawing room; D: dining room
Ground floor	E: front parlour; F: breakfast room
Basement	G: kitchens and service areas.

Even in modern houses the most important room, used for family relaxing and entertaining guests, has the largest window.

Lighting

Pupils will have realised from their own homes that houses are lit both by artificial and natural light. In the past the aim was to make maximum use of the natural light available. South-facing rooms get more light than north-facing rooms and for longer; they also tend to be warmer. South-facing rooms with large windows were therefore the lightest and most comfortable in the house. In this way the size and placing of the windows was linked to the size and status of the room. Pupils can use the windows to help them identify which rooms were the most prestigious, which were designed for the family and which were used by servants or for storage.

Windows allowed light in but, unless they were protected in some way, they also let heat out. Although window glass was used in Roman Britain, its use in domestic houses was exceptional until the sixteenth century and it was not until the eighteenth century that it became widespread. People used what materials they could to give them some protection from the weather, like oiled parchment and paper, or thin slices of horn, and those who could afford it would have had internal wooden shutters.

Before gas and later electric lights were available people relied on candlelight, oil or rush lights and firelight to illuminate their rooms.

Lights would be moved around as and where they were needed. Get your pupils to think how different this would have been to modern lighting: it would have been less bright, subject to flickering, and giving off a distinctive smoky or oily smell. Gas lighting became affordable on a wide scale at the end of the nineteenth century, and electric lighting followed about thirty years later. Not many houses have retained their gas light fittings, but wall switches for electric lights often remain, and are interesting for pupils to note because they reflect the design trends of their times.

Heating and cooking

Just as the size of the windows indicates the status and function of the room, so too does the level of the heating provision. Until the last century most houses had open fires which means that fireplaces, hearths, ranges, chimneys or louvres, or traces of them, may have survived. Decorated fireplaces indicate prestigious accommodation; large, plain ones are found in kitchens, and there may be none at all in storage, service or servants' areas.

Underfloor heating was used first by the Romans, and generally not again until the nineteenth century. Very often, all that can be seen at Roman sites are the stacks of tiles which held up the floor and around which the hot air circulated, and the remains of the furnace at one end. The Romans also heated their walls by embedding box flues, square clay pipes, through which hot air was drawn upwards.

Fireplaces showing the different status and functions of rooms in the same house – the top picture is from a bedroom and the bottom from the kitchen. From the Little Castle, Bolsover, Derbyshire.

Today heating and cooking are separate activities; in many but the homes of the wealthy they were not; large fireplaces, as well as being used to heat a room, may also have provided people with cooking facilities and hot water. Medieval built-in ovens were originally separate from the fireplace, and appear as large spherical shapes within the thickness of the wall. Twigs were burnt inside them, which, when the surrounding oven walls were hot, were removed and food cooked in the retained heat. By the eighteenth century, cast iron ranges included both fire and cooking apparatus.

The Victorian cast iron range was used for heating water and cooking.

On unfurnished or ruined sites, pupils will be able to distinguish between kitchen fireplaces and others by their greater size and plainness. If the fireplace surround has disappeared, the back of the grate may still be recognisable by tiles set on edge in a herringbone pattern. Tiles were used because ordinary stone shattered in the heat, but tiles, which had already been fired in manufacture, did not.

Water supply and sanitation

Water might be available from a nearby natural supply, like a spring, stream or an underground source accessed by a well. Otherwise it was collected, delivered by water carriers, or brought in through pipes. Some Roman villas had piped water and drainage provision, with sophisticated washing and sanitation systems. Great medieval houses might have piped water as well, but this was for kitchen and washing use, not for carrying away human waste.

Large medieval dwellings will usually have evidence of a water supply, often a well. Lavatories, known as garderobes, were simply holes which jutted out over the walls, where the waste piled up

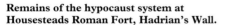

Remains of the hypocaust system at Housesteads Roman Fort, Hadrian's Wall.

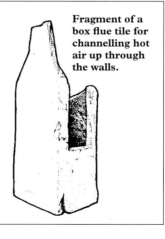

Fragment of a box flue tile for channelling hot air up through the walls.

until removed, or, in castles, fell into the moat. Garderobes indicate that the adjoining room was high-ranking personal accommodation – servants went outside. Very grand accommodation had garderobes which were entered via a small storage room for clothes called the wardrobe, as the ammoniacal smell deterred moths. Most medieval monasteries were nearly always sited near to streams, both to supply water and carry away waste: look out for evidence of lavatories lying over a stream, culvert, or drain, which may now be dry.

Piped water was gradually supplied to the houses firstly of

Two seater garderobe and chutes through which waste was deposited outside at Orford Castle in Suffolk.

the rich, then to groups of houses where water had to be fetched from the communal tap, then by this century, to every home bar those in remote locations.

All fixed evidence of domestic sanitary arrangements disappeared from most houses between the fifteenth and eighteenth centuries because people relied on chamber

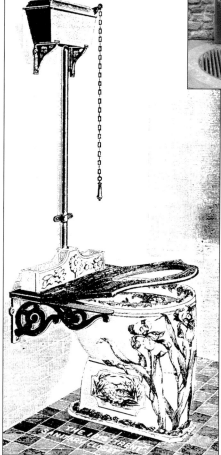

Miner having a bath; first part of this century.

Pump, Great Yarmouth.

Victorian flush lavatories were more highly decorated than modern ones.

pots or close stools, which had a seat containing a pot that could be emptied. Outside lavatories, which had to have their contents removed periodically, were still in use in rural areas and by the poor in this century, but bathrooms with piped water and flush toilets were being installed into better-off homes in Victorian times.

Pupils can search for clues to the way in which water was brought to the house they are studying, and how waste was taken away. Is there a well, stream, drains? If a stream was being used for both drinking water and waste disposal, where would the kitchen be in relation to the lavatory, up- or downstream? Are there taps upstairs and downstairs, or a pump? They can look for waste pipes on the external walls, and note to which room they connect. Why were outside lavatories well away from the house? How would the family wash? How was water heated? How was it transported and disposed of?

HOW WAS IT BUILT?

The walls of any substantial building have to support the weight of the roof: this puts a pressure or force onto them which they have to be strong enough to withstand. The weight of the roof is carried in one of two ways: either by the whole wall or by a framework. If the whole wall takes the strain, it needs to be constructed of material which is very robust. If a framework is used, then the frame has to be strong, but the spaces can be filled in with anything, as long as it is rigid and

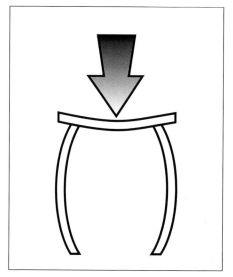

Forces acting on the walls of a house.

proof against wind and water. Early timber-framed buildings were made in an inverted V shape, from trees with curved trunks. They are called cruck buildings, and usually have side walls added to them.

The way in which the wall is constructed affects the shape of the openings in it. Loadbearing walls are weakened by gaps; the full force of weight suddenly has no support, and the whole thing can collapse.

A cruck cottage.

The tops of windows and doors are reinforced by strong lintels, or, in old buildings where the walls were made strong by being very thick, arches were found to be the strongest shape to take the weight.

In framework walls, the openings can generally be as large as the frame allows, as they are only supporting the weight of the infill above them.

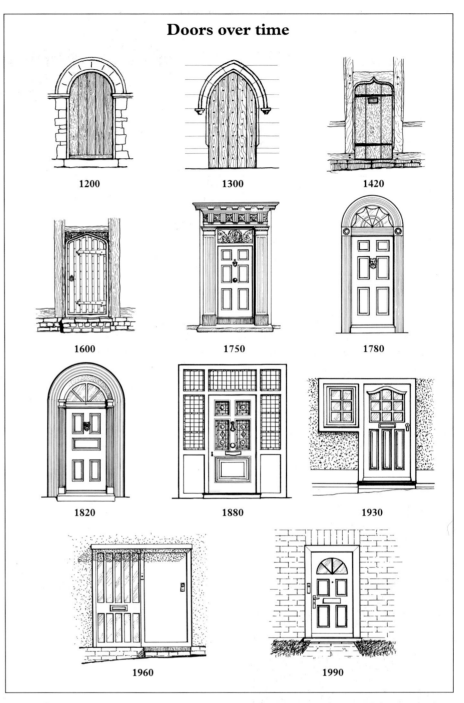

Doors over time

1200   1300   1420

1600   1750   1780

1820   1880   1930

1960   1990

WHY WAS IT BUILT? WHY WAS IT BUILT HERE?

Houses can be built for a number of reasons: to keep people safe, as a place to show off one's wealth, as a place of work, as a home for a large family or to do all these things. Someone who wanted a safe place to live would obviously be looking for a different sort of site from someone who wanted a country house where they could entertain their friends.

Pupils will need to search for clues in the setting as well as in the house. To feel safe, the owner may have built on top of a hill so that there was a good view of anyone approaching, which is why castle builders often chose high places. Today, people may want to feel safe from an invasion of privacy, in which case a secluded, hidden spot is best. In the eighteenth and nineteenth centuries, rich people took to building their grand houses away from the noise and dirt of city life, but near enough to travel to their business when necessary. At the other end of the scale, housing was built for

workers by employers, just so that they were near their places of work. Pupils will need to remember that the landscape may have changed since the house was built so they will need to consult historic atlases, aerial photographs and maps.

WHEN WAS IT BUILT? WHEN WAS IT CHANGED?

Pupils can try to decide if they think the house is older or younger than the house they live in, or other houses in the town or village

Windows over time

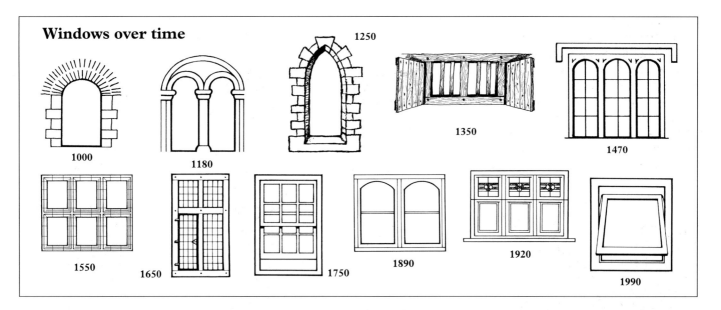

around them. The shape of windows and doors is a good indication of the date of a building, but they are also the features which get most often updated. Houses are constantly being modified to meet new needs and new demands.

Alterations can reflect a need for more space, more status, keeping up with fashion, or a change of use in the building. Others are aimed at adding more comfort and convenience, like installing central heating, modern plumbing and double glazing. Modifications can also be made to give a structure a longer life; houses can be sand blasted, underpinned, pebble dashed, or clad in order to prevent deterioration.

Changes in brick and stonework, lines of old arches and bricked up fireplaces or windows, new looking pipes and different shaped windows can all provide valuable clues about changes which have taken place over the years. Pupils

Looking at change

Label the pictures of this house from 1 to 6 in date order

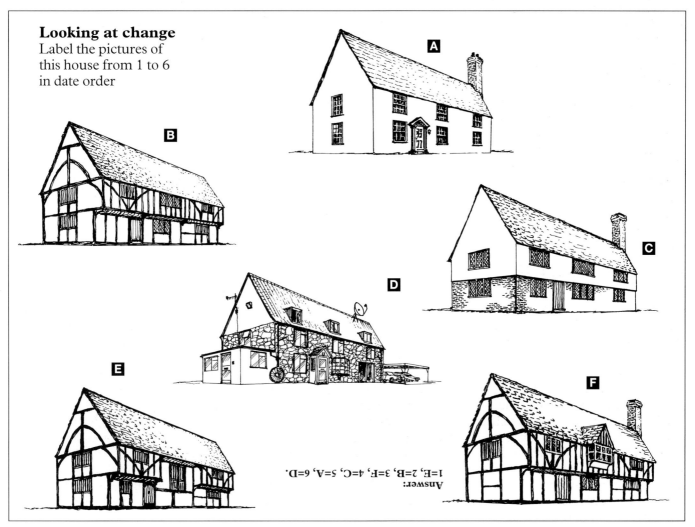

Answer:
1=E, 2=B, 3=F, 4=C, 5=A, 6=D.

Which words describe each house?

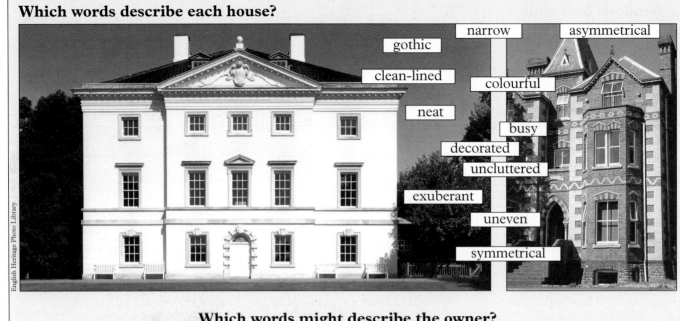

narrow   asymmetrical

gothic

clean-lined   colourful

neat

busy

decorated

uncluttered

exuberant

uneven

symmetrical

Which words might describe the owner?
fussy neat dynamic elegant rich very rich tidy energetic calm ordered vigorous jolly cool

can try and decide which of these came first. Use the six houses on the previous page to show them the process by asking them to put them in chronological order.

Another form of change occurs through decay. Pupils can look for evidence of this. The obvious signs are when the brick or stone work has begun to crumble and fall, but pupils could also look for moss or lichen growing on the walls, for discolouration of the stone and for pock marks in it. Any decorative carvings on the house may well have begun to lose their definition or to have fallen away. Cracks in the paintwork, woodwork or plasterwork can often be seen and the internal decorations may have faded owing to too much exposure to light.

WHO LIVED HERE?
The architectural style of a house and how it is decorated can tell us a great deal about contemporary fashions and about the taste, lifestyle and aspirations of the occupier. The shape and style of the windows and doors in many houses can also play a part in the decoration of the house. The windows in Georgian houses have been used to add detail, balance and symmetry as well as to let in light.

The decor is much the easiest

Differences in status can easily be seen between the family's and the servant's parts of the house, even is a structure as functional as stairs. These are from Bolsover Little Castle, Derbyshire: The stairs on the left were for family and those on the right were for servants.

thing to change for any new owners wishing to place their own mark on a property, but fashionable alterations sometimes make it very difficult to find out how a house might have looked originally.

Just by looking at a house from the outside pupils can draw up a list of words to describe it, and from there words which describe in a very general way the status and taste of the person who originally lived in it.

The size and how the internal space is organised gives clues to how many people lived there, and what they did. Floor plans of the house can be used to find out how the different rooms are linked to each other and how people moved through them. In a furnished house it will be easy to see what each

room was used for, but in an empty or ruined one pupils will have to work out the function of the rooms for themselves. They can form some idea of what a particular room is used for from its size and its position in relation to other rooms in the building. Rooms for living in, formal rooms and storage rooms tend to be larger than rooms used for sleeping in. Kitchens are near food storage areas, and bathrooms near bedrooms, just as they are in houses today. The exception to this is that kitchens in medieval and great country houses were usually well away from the formal eating rooms, to lessen the risk from fire and prevent noise and smells reaching the family and their guests. The most important areas are the most finely decorated and well lit, while storage space or servants' rooms are much less so.

One way of introducing this idea to pupils is to get them to go round rooms in school, such as the headteacher's office, their own classroom, the lavatories, and the hall to find which is the most prestigious. They should give marks out of ten for quality of heating provision, size, furniture, window size, and wall and floor covering. They can apply the same criteria to discover the prestige rooms and the working areas on site.

BUILDING MATERIALS

The materials chosen to build a house depend on a whole range of things: expense, proximity, availability, and the sophistication of the technology needed to gather, shape, manufacture, transport or handle them.

Before canal, rail and road transport solved the problem of carrying heavy goods cheaply, most houses were built of whatever was available nearby. This gave rise to regional differences; in East Anglia where there was hardly any good building stone, timber-framed or flint houses predominated, whereas in Northamptonshire, ironstone gives buildings their distinctive dark brown colour. Only the rich could afford to transport heavy building stone over a long distance.

Early houses, or the houses of the poor, were usually made of materials which were cheap, easy to handle and readily available. Wood, clay, thatch and turves were most often used. Cob, a mixture of wet clay, chopped straw, chalk if it was available and small pebbles and sand, which set hard, was also cheap and easy to obtain. Cob walls were coated to make them waterproof, and were protected from damp at the base by stone foundations, and at the top by thatch, which provided eaves which sheltered the walls from rain.

Timber-framed buildings were usually infilled with wattle and daub, which is twigs woven round stouter wooden uprights and plastered over with a mixture of mud, straw and, sometimes, dung. Bricks were also used, fitted into a herringbone pattern.

Heavy, rigid materials could only be handled in relatively small pieces, so how these were fixed together became an important factor in their overall strength. The bonding agent, mortar, was important, as was the pattern in which the pieces were laid. Mortar uses lime as an ingredient, so limepits and limekilns are often found nearby. The most prestigious building material was stone cut into

In the 1930s there was a fashion for houses made with cement walls, which could be moulded into curved shapes.

Flint.

Brick and cobbles.

Bricks – modern are larger than old ones.

Ashlar or stone in cut blocks.

Stone rubble.

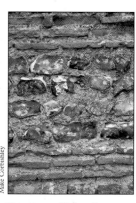

Roman wall showing bonding layers of thin Roman bricks.

A thatcher at work and the tools of his trade.

dash, timber boarding, and tiles.

Pupils do not have to be experts in building techniques in order to be able to find out about what the house they are studying was made of, and from there how it was constructed. They can do a survey on the types of materials used, looking to see what intrinsic properties make them a good choice for that particular job, or what techniques have been used to make them suitable. More simply, they can list the natural and man-made materials or look to see what materials have been used inside and what outside and why.

WHO BUILT THE HOUSE?

Many different people are involved in building a structure. As a follow-on from looking at building

regular blocks. This was called ashlar, and was often used to make the two faces of the wall, with rubble filling up the central space. This and other techniques are often more clearly seen in ruined houses where the walls are breaking down.

When bricks became widely available, they were often the preferred material, and could be laid in a variety of patterns. In modern houses, they are often backed by cheaper breeze blocks, made of a cement-like compound. Cement

Thatch.

Stone flags, which get smaller the closer the are to the ridge.

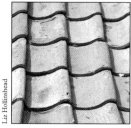

Manufactured pantiles.

Slates.

Handmade tiles.

Concrete tiles.

Old crafts sometimes die out. When English Heritage wanted to repair a cob building, experiments had to be made with different mixtures and techniques. Here the cob is being consolidated in a wooden frame the width of a wall.

was used in some Roman building, as were thin bricks (often called tiles). There are a few cement houses, but re-enforced cement is used more widely in steel-framed buildings, like blocks of flats.

Roofs are also made of a vast variety of materials, some water proof, like slate and tiles, and others only useful by being managed properly, like thatch, which is long wheatstraw or Norfolk reeds, arranged lengthways so that water runs down them. Thatched roofs need a steep pitch, as much as 75 degrees, whilst modern materials can be as little as 20 degrees.

It is more difficult to see what a house has been made of when it has been covered for protective or decorative purposes. There are many types of renders, such as stucco, ordinary plaster, pebble-

materials encourage pupils to think about all the different tasks which would have needed to be done and the range of labourers and craftspeople who would have performed them. They might try and work out the order in which they think the jobs would have been done and then they can do some research into this back at school to see if they were right. Encourage them to go back to fundamentals, like the quarrying and carting of stone to the site. The local museum may have a selection of tools different craftsmen used: ask if they are available on loan.

STRATEGIES FOR LOOKING AT SITES

This section contains practical ideas for use in class and on site. Most of the suggestions can be simplified or be made more sophisticated, depending on the age range you are teaching, except for Key Stage 1, for whom there is a separate section.

BEFORE THE VISIT

If you intend to study a house which is formally open to the public, the guide book will usually include floor plans. These are very useful in giving an overall bird's eye view of the layout, but if your pupils have not come across scaled plans before, they will need help to understand them before the visit.

Beg a showhouse brochure from an estate agent. These contain floor plans which you can use with your class to put together an identi-kit picture of the family who might live there. Then introduce the plans for the house you will be visiting and repeat the exercise. This provides a good opening for talking about other lifestyles. It also starts the topic off very firmly as something to do with people, which will help your pupils to imagine what it might have been like to live in different circumstances.

Alternatively, ask your class for a list of the rooms, and their functions, in an ordinary family-sized dwelling. Use this as a starting point for introducing the differences in the lifestyle of the period you want to study. For example, if the house you want to investigate was of high social status, you can introduce the fact that servants, extended family and semi-permanent guests were the norm. Pupils can be helped to piece together what accommodation members of the household would have needed in which to sleep, socialise and work. In large community dwellings in which food and drink were processed on the

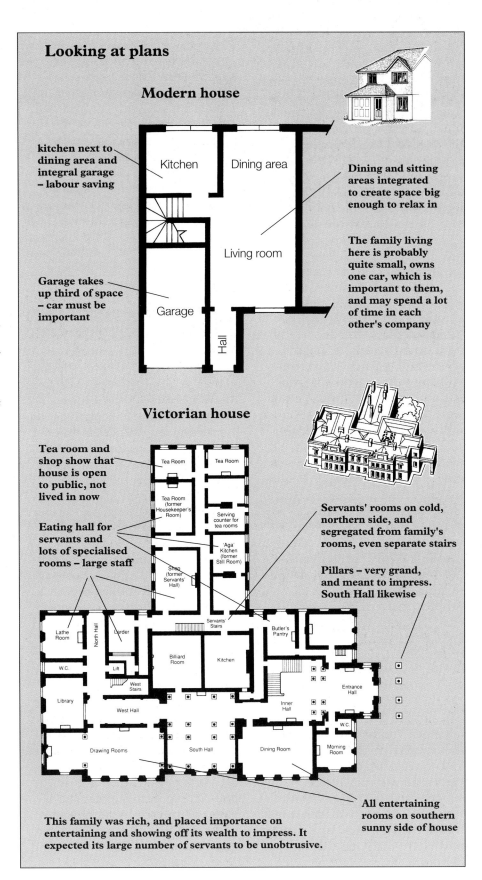

Looking at plans

Modern house

kitchen next to dining area and integral garage – labour saving

Kitchen

Dining area

Dining and sitting areas integrated to create space big enough to relax in

Living room

The family living here is probably quite small, owns one car, which is important to them, and may spend a lot of time in each other's company

Garage takes up third of space – car must be important

Garage

Hall

Victorian house

Tea room and shop show that house is open to public, not lived in now

Tea Room

Tea Room

Tea Room (former Housekeeper's Room)

Serving counter for tea rooms

Eating hall for servants and lots of specialised rooms – large staff

'Aga' Kitchen (former Still Room)

Shop (former Servants' Hall)

Servants' rooms on cold, northern side, and segregated from family's rooms, even separate stairs

Servants' Stairs

Butler's Pantry

Pillars – very grand, and meant to impress. South Hall likewise

Lathe Room

North Hall

Larder

Billiard Room

Kitchen

W.C.

Lift

West Stairs

Entrance Hall

Library

West Hall

Inner Hall

W.C.

Drawing Rooms

South Hall

Dining Room

Morning Room

All entertaining rooms on southern sunny side of house

This family was rich, and placed importance on entertaining and showing off its wealth to impress. It expected its large number of servants to be unobtrusive.

premises, there would have been outhouses for brewing, baking and storage. The list will help during the visit in understanding the domestic organisation, and it will also alert pupils to notice if any rooms which they might expect to find are missing, like bathrooms, and promote enquiry as to why.

If you are doing a general local study of housing, you will probably only have access to exteriors. Even if you are allowed inside, it is still useful to spend time extracting as much information as possible from the outside. Use pictures of house exteriors to introduce your class to the idea of looking for clues to the interior arrangements. Better still if you can, take some photographs of the same house from all sides and use those. Window sizes will help in deciding which are the important rooms, but the position of the door and chimney stack (if it is an old house) will also give a good idea of interior layout, as will drainage pipes.

It is useful to bring in small samples of building material: bricks; building stone; a chip of breeze block; roofing and flooring slates and tiles; long sections of straw; mortar; wood; glass (protected round the edges); steel; nails, or whatever you can find. It does not matter if the pieces are broken, as this often reveals more information about the material. The local museum may be able to help out with old materials if you want them, like Tudor bricks or Roman tiles.

Get pupils to look closely at the materials by sorting them into groups, giving their criteria. Classifications could include: natural or manufactured; durable or perishable; rigid or malleable; or by function – used in walls, roof, floor, windows, or door. With the help of a magnifying glass, accurate descriptions for each item can be compiled. On site, this will help them to recognise materials and look to see how and why they have been used. On ruined sites they will be more able to assess what is missing, and to look for evidence of it, so that they can build up a picture of what the place may have looked like originally.

Looking at the outside

A lot can be discovered about the inside of this house from looking closely at the exterior. The best upstairs and downstairs rooms are likely to be those with the biggest windows; in this house those with the bay windows. The central chimney stack shows that these two rooms, and probably the ones behind them have fireplaces. The central flue means that the stairs are not on the central wall, so they are likely to be on the side wall. A look at the side reveals a window at between-storey level, which indicates a landing window. This window is also decorated with coloured glass, a common feature of landing windows. This means that the stairs lead off from the hall. The small window at the front is frosted, which indicates

Liz Hollinshead

a bathroom. The pipes at the side confirm this.

INVESTIGATING AND RECORDING ON SITE

There is generally so much information offered by a visit that it may be best to home in onto one or two themes and concentrate on those. For example, looking at the construction or materials used, or what cooking facilities there were, or collecting clues to build up a picture of the people who lived there. Alternatively, if you have enough adult helpers, you can make groups responsible for gathering information about various areas, and then share this later in the visit, or back in class.

Getting pupils to slow down and look really closely can usually be better achieved by asking for labelled drawings rather than written notes. If notes are taken, allow pupils to jot down words or phrases; they can spend time writing up proper sentences back in class. If you prefer drawings, emphasise that these are different from artwork, and are for recording accurate, detailed information. According to ability or age range, they should include notes about approximate size, colours, textures, or materials. Different groups can record windows, doors, walls, and roof on the outside, and if an

approximate scale is agreed beforehand these can be made into a composite picture later.

Inside, you can prevent over-crowding by deploying different groups to sketch wall and floor coverings, ceiling designs, doors, fireplaces, and any other fittings, which can later be integrated into a catalogue of period design. Alternatively, assign five pupils to a room to each sketch one wall or the floor, and present this as designers in the past did, as a net. If the house is empty, this can be used in class for researching and adding in wall and floor coverings, fittings, and furniture. They will need to agree on a scale first. Furnished houses give a great deal more information than unfurnished ones, but there are drawbacks: there may be too much for pupils to take in, and you may be unable to stop for long in any one place in case the class obstructs the normal visitor flow. You may be able to get round this by explaining to the custodian during your planning visit what work you want to do, and asking for advice.

If you want a record of the outside of the house, draw an outline of the facades you want onto A3 paper, cut them in half, photocopy and hand out halves to each pupil. On site ask them to fill it in with all the details they can see, and then pair up the halves at random so pupils can see how accurately they have recorded positions of windows and rooflines. According to the abilities of your class you may want to mark in the levels of each storey first, or leave out the outline altogether and just indicate the roof and ground levels. If all the sides are drawn, and if the house is a regular shape, these can be mounted on card, joined and reinforced at the corners, and made into three dimensional, if roofless, models.

Photographs do not always pick up fine detail, which is why archaeologists always produce drawings of the finds from their excavations. If you want pupils to make close-up records of details of decorative work, for example, a long shot

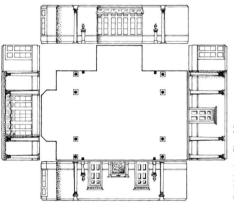

Robert Adam recorded his design for the dining room at Audley End, Essex in the form of a net.

photograph, and carefully worked drawings, are a good combination. They can all be pinned on the classroom wall later with string pointers connecting the drawings to the relevant places on the photograph.

Small, hand-held tape recorders or dictaphones are useful for note taking in furnished houses, where clip boards may not be allowed. They can also be used to produce your own audio guide to the site.

SITE WORK STRATEGIES

Work for a site visit can be based on the framework of questions suggested in the preceding chapter. Groups of pupils can be responsible for investigating how the

house has been designed, how it has been built and what materials have been used in its construction, who lived there, why it was built and when. They can present their findings to the rest of the class on site, and should be prepared to answer questions. They may also need to keep a separate list of things that can only be fully understood by research back at school. This is a good way of covering the whole site, and of giving individuals a feeling of being an expert on one particular aspect.

Problem solving

Problem solving is an effective strategy in encouraging close observation and analysis of the surviving evidence. An imaginary situation is created in which pupils need to work together to deliver a plan which will produce a

The dining room, Audley End House.

satisfactory outcome. For example, if the main focus is on what the house looked like when it was built, suggest a scenario in which the house is to be used in a television costume drama. Your pupils are to be in charge of this project, and need to make a list of all the items that have to be removed before filming begins, and any that they think should be introduced. They should also make suggestions for hiding any remaining modern features. This can be done on the first visit if you are confident that pupils will recognise what is modern and what original, but you can use it as a basis for further research and visits if you want them to check less immediately dateable

items, like furniture, place settings or kitchen utensils.

If you want to look at how space was organised, put your pupils into the role of estate agents from the appropriate period, with the problem of selling the house. Look at advertisements and brochures in class before the visit so that a list of tasks can be drawn up, like describing the house, its rooms and its situation, and measuring each room, deciding what its function is and what its good and bad points are. Sketches or photographs will be needed. This is also a good opportunity to look at the use of words, and examine the use of emotive language.

To encourage an investigation of the design or fabric of the building, you might suggest that a publishing company has decided to produce a new book on design and decoration in the past. It wants to show how different materials have been used over the centuries to create different effects. There will be sections on stone carving, glazing, plaster work, textiles, painting, and wood carving, or whatever it is that the house you are looking at is rich in. Pupils can be asked to help with this book by choosing a section they would like to work on and preparing notes and drawings for the editor.

Investigating display techniques

Asking pupils to create their own way of displaying the house not only focuses their attention on how the house functioned, but also encourages them to think about the way in which physical evidence is presented and interpreted.

For any presentation device, pupils need to think about what audience they are targeting, as this will dictate language level, and the sophistication of information. For this reason, it is a good idea to suggest an audience of their peers, or younger people.

It may be that your class will want to redesign the method of presenting information that already exists. In unfurnished or ruined houses, this is usually conveyed on interpretation panels. These give

Most houses will provide a variety of wall coverings, floors and ceilings. These are from the seventeenth-century house known as the Little Castle, Bolsover, Derbyshire.

Ceiling designs.

Wall coverings.

Flooring materials.

the salient facts, and also often include an artist's impression of what the place looked like when it was lived in. Your class can make up their own panels, with the information which they consider most interesting, and their own pictures. The pictures can either be the site as it is now, or their own reconstruction of what it might have looked like. For this they need to make detailed drawings on site, then in school research furniture, fittings, and costume(if people are to be included) which they can add into the sketch.

Guide books and audio tapes can be prepared. The most efficient way to organise this is to make groups responsible for different rooms or aspects: they will need to decide together what information they want to give, then each member can contribute a couple of sentences about different features, like furniture, wall and floor coverings, windows, doors, pictures, how the room was used, and so on. To encourage precision, limit the number of words or time that should be spent on each description.

Scripts can be written for straightforward guided tours, or for tours written for actors in costume. In the latter case pupils will need to decide on the characters involved, and what rooms would be associated with each. They might also draw up sketches for the costume, or for token costume, like a hat.

Your pupils may want to create a totally different way of displaying the site. For example, they may realise that one element which is missing from most presentations is background sound. They will need to think about what would be heard in the room: a clock ticking, fire crackling, cooking and household tasks being carried out, doors opening, snatches of conversation, food being eaten. The sounds can be reproduced with impromptu devices or their own voices, and then recorded.

More radically, pupils may want to sacrifice visitor comfort in order to present the site more authentically. Houses which are open to visitors generally have a level of background heating and lighting which does not reflect the living conditions of the inhabitants, and room displays may be arranged to facilitate visitor flow. Pupils can note down all the extra devices which are purely for modern visitor comfort and safety, and make decisions about what changes are feasible, and what extra precautions will be needed to ensure the safety of the viewing public.

Some visitors may not be able to see the site very well but they can

Even the most realistic setting can be made more life-like with the addition of background noise and smells, or the detritus of everyday living.

enjoy it in other ways. A "Please touch" guide to the house could be prepared which will introduce visitors to all the different materials which have been used to build it. Pupils could devise a textured plan of the site on which the route for partially-sighted visitors is marked.

The position and size of features need to be noted by labelled drawings, as do the texture, colour and patterns of the materials used. To ensure that all the information is collected, it is probably best to make groups responsible for recording different parts, like each facade, the structural shapes, the walls and whatever is on them, the roof, all the windows, the doors.

PRESENTATION

Thinking big can be fun and impressive. Measure enough wallpaper to cover any large areas of classroom wall, and put aside the same amount. Give one lot to pupils to paint in a door, and the other to another group to paint in the interior which would have been seen behind the door. When they have finished, cut round the door on three sides, so that it opens. It helps if a metre rule is used to make a straight crease in the remaining side. Paste and staple the two sheets together and stick onto the wall. The same idea of parts which open – doors, windows, even the whole front walls of rooms, can be used to show both exterior and interiors. Use potato, lino or string printing to pick out the pattern of the walls and roof.

Drawings can be worked up to form a happy families-type card game. If you have been following a local studies topic, four features from each house investigated can

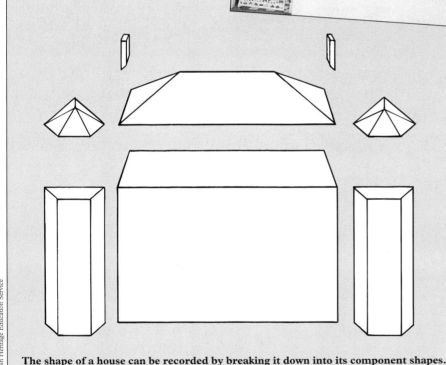

The shape of a house can be recorded by breaking it down into its component shapes.

Information or touch points can be indicated, and the script for an audio tape prepared for each point.

Model making requires a degree of accuracy which calls on sophisticated recording and mathematical skills. Most buildings can be broken down into component shapes, from which the model can then be built. These should be estimated or measured, and the ways in which they relate to the whole recorded.

If you are contemplating doing a model showing the interior, then you will need groups to record each room. Back in class a scale should be agreed upon, and each group can decide together on the materials and method of making the features which they studied. The facade recording group can act as quality controllers, managers, and the decision-making body on the positioning of each part.

be redrawn on to thick paper or card the size of playing cards. If only one house has been studied, select four things from each room, or if the exterior only was inves-

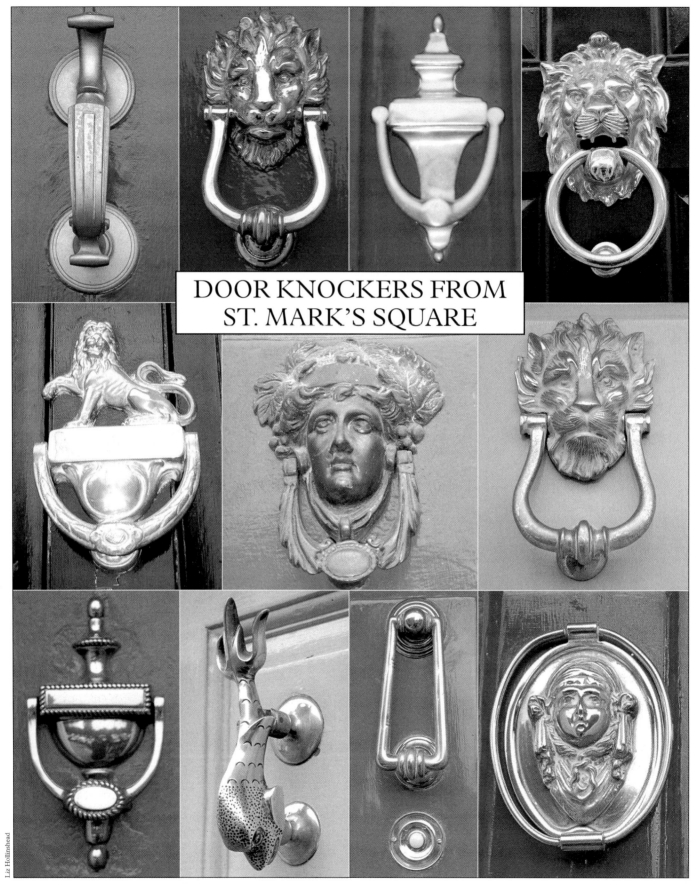

DOOR KNOCKERS FROM
ST. MARK'S SQUARE

Liz Hollinshead

Images of door knockers made into a poster.

tigated, four different materials, four different shaped windows, four items of door furniture or decoration, four roof items(shape, roofing and capping tiles, chimney, guttering, barge boards), four details of the railings or front gate, and so on. The backs of the cards can be printed with a design inspired by the house.

Labelled drawings can be pinned on the wall around the ground plan or a large picture of the house, or used in their own, word processed guide to the site. Both will require explanations and descriptions.

Drawings made on site in pencil and labelled with detailed colour notes can be redone in a different, coloured, medium and made into posters for the site. Posters of rows of doors and windows have been commercial successes. Pupils could do similar ones, or choose another feature, again in rows, like door knockers, or chimney pots.

In medieval times they did not have baked beans and today we do not have peacocks or boars heads. They did not have electric cookers they had spits and cauldrons and fires.

Liz Hollinshead

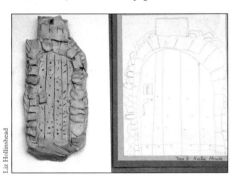

Liz Hollinshead

Decorative features can look good when reproduced in clay, again using the labelled drawings made on site. Ornamental chimneys, friezes, and door knockers can look spectacular in clay which has been painted and fired or left to harden.

KEY STAGE 1

Key Stage 1 pupils need a different way of working. Start with a story that all the class is likely to know, *The Three Little Pigs* or *Hansel and Gretel*, and explore with them why a house made of straw or gingerbread is not going to be successful. Bring in straw, twigs or ginger biscuits and a house brick. Get the pupils to place them outside and check them together the next morning. If the straw and twigs have blown away, or the biscuit is sodden, the point will have been made. There are opportunities for vocabulary work, like suggesting labels for the materials, and for comparisons, like hardest, heaviest, softer. Tease out from pupils the function of different features by asking what it would be like if we had no roofs, windows or doors, and ask them what these are made of, and why.

Despite the fact that they may live in flats, bungalows or terraces, most Key Stage 1 pupils, when

asked, will draw a standard, square, detached house. Capitalise on this by using it to re-enforce shape recognition. Use different coloured card and cut squares for the body of the house, triangles for the roof, rectangles for the windows, chimney and door, and small circles for the door knobs, and write the word describing the shape on each. You can use this simply as a colour and shape matching exercise, by asking them to make up their own picture using an already completed set as a guide, or you can make a beetle-like game for them to play. Numbering each different feature from one to six (house front, roof, chimney, window, door, door knob), let them throw a die in turn until they have built up a house. The usual rules apply, windows cannot be taken until they have got the house front to put them on, and the roof has to be collected before the chimney.

On the visit, or during a walk in the locality, ask pupils to look for the shapes and encourage them to notice that not all houses are square and detached, or roofs triangular. Also ask if all walls are brick, and if not, what are they like – hard, rough, coloured, patterned. If you are looking at houses near the school, which may all be designed on the same pattern, get pupils to look carefully for the differences; this may only be in door design or colour, but it is a good lesson in slowing down and looking closely, and in realising differences and similarities.

It helps to have a theme in mind if you plan to visit a furnished house, like lighting or heating, which pupils will know about in their own homes. Get them to talk about the differences between then and now – appearance, size, and how it works, and if possible, ask an adult helper to write down some of their ideas, so that you can remind them about it in class. They might enjoy collecting bits and pieces from home to form their own class

English Heritage Education Service

museum on the topic, candlesticks, a light bulb or switch, an oil lamp, a lump of coal, fireirons, pictures of electric fires or chandeliers. Lighting a candle in a darkened room is an effective way of glimpsing lighting provision in the past.

If you visit a ruined or unfurnished house look at window or door shapes, and ask how they differ from modern ones. See how many different examples can be found, and, if you have a camera, record the different shapes and use the photographs together with pictures of modern equivalents in a sorting exercise back in school. The differences in room sizes can also be compared to modern ones, which will help to demonstrate that people had a different lifestyle in the past.

Follow this up by bringing in pictures of modern dwellings, and those from the past, and interior illustrations. Ask firstly whether the subject of the picture is modern or old, and then ask on what clues the decision was based. After talking about the pictures, lead pupils into sorting them into new, old and very old.

USING DIFFERENT FORMS OF EVIDENCE

Site work and research feed into and inform each other. The strength of site work is that it enables pupils to study primary evidence at first hand, and it generates questions and stimulates interest. But for the answers to some of these questions, like who lived there, other sources may have to be consulted.

PHYSICAL EVIDENCE

Pupils need to be aware that buildings can change, both inside and out, so that they know that the building they see may not be identical to the original one.

Additions to the original building

Houses are not static; bits are added on over time to meet the different needs of occupants and changing uses. Very often later buildings are designed to blend with the original therefore it may be difficult to clearly identify phases of construction.

Missing buildings

As well as adding to buildings, sections may well have been pulled down. Very often previous buildings within the site will have disappeared, as a result of rebuilding or damage. Close observation may reveal foundations, the lines of former walls, roofs and staircases, which pupils can use to piece together the stages of development of the site. When there are no traces of remains, a biased interpretation of the site can result. For example, many of the workshops and stables attached to medieval dwellings were made of wood, which over time decayed and completely vanished, or the outside lavatories from terraced houses have been pulled down and the yard cemented over. The assumption could be made that horses were tethered in the open, and no activities like smithing

or brewing took place in the medieval household, or that terraced houses had no lavatories.

Changes in the surrounding area

A house exists within the context of the surrounding area. A once prestigious building set in its own spacious gardens may now be dwarfed by industrial buildings or be surrounded by a housing estate because the local population has changed or the environment altered. Comparing the existing evidence against old maps, pictures, photographs and accounts will help pupils to see how the surrounding area has changed, and how and why the house has been altered.

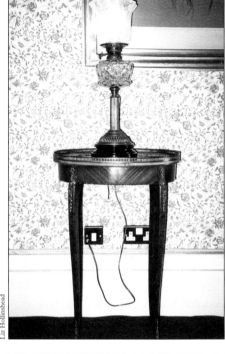

Liz Hollinshead

Liz Hollinshead

Liz Hollinshead

Presentation

Houses which are open to the public often need to be adapted to provide a safe, informative and enjoyable experience for the visitor. This might include the addition of signs and labels, interpretation panels, railings and barriers, and protective carpets or glass in the windows. It might be more convenient for the managers to establish a visitor route that would not have been that taken by an original inhabitant or guest, and the furniture might have to be arranged artificially so that it does not

obstruct it. Pleasant heating and lighting levels will be provided for visitor comfort which bear no relation to that experienced by the inhabitants. Houses from which all the furniture has been lost may be refurnished from other sources, perhaps with pristine replica items.

Pupils should be made aware of these techniques so that they can take them into consideration when they are trying to find out what the place may have been like originally, and what the living conditions were for its inhabitants.

Debate about different interpretive methods and recreation of the past is an interesting topic for discussion after a visit. Points raised might include:

■ should modern facilities, like lavatories, car parks and cafes be installed at the expense of original features?

■ how far should modern materials, techniques, and replicas be used? Evidence is often missing, in particular about the lives of servants or the poorer classes. How can this be shown?

■ in an old house, what period of its history should be represented in the furnishings?

■ should guesses be made for parts of the story that are missing?

■ historians may disagree about the facts and how they should be presented – more than one inter-pretation may exist. Should visitors be given several explanations, or is this too confusing?

PICTORIAL RESOURCES

Try to ensure wherever possible that all sources have dates, author-ship and information which will allow them to be placed in context.

Contemporary drawings

Pupils should be aware the artist may have wanted to please the owner by leaving out unsightly bits, or may have added a romantic gloss. Pupils can find the spot from which the artist worked, and compare the picture with what is there now. They need to think how reliable it is as a record: if, for example, it includes a part which has since disappeared, but the rest is faithful to what remains, it can probably be trusted.

Photographs

A photograph can contain impor-tant detail about the site and the people who lived and worked there, allowing comparison with today. However, photographs can be posed, with interiors arranged to portray a particular image, or

people dressed in their best clothes standing in formal stances rather than naturally working or playing. Photographs of exteriors can give valuable information, not just about the house but also about the immediate surroundings, like a street, that will help in imagining what it was like to live there. If you take a photograph to the site, get pupils to talk about the extra information it gives, and if possible, take a camera so that a picture can be taken from the same spot as a record. If there are people on the original photograph, ask pupils to pose in the same position. This will help them in judging how natural the original was, and also give them a starting point in looking at the differences between then and now.

Maps and plans

Old maps and plans can be com-pared with modern ones to show how a house and its environment have changed over a period of time. Maps of the surrounding areas can also be used to see if changes there might have influenced alterations to the site and also to put the house into a broader context.

WRITTEN MATERIAL

Census returns

These give a great deal of infor-mation about the people who lived in a house, and can be obtained from local history libraries. They are useful in adding the human dimension to a house. The census was taken every ten years from 1841, and notes who was living in every property, where they were born, and, if adult, what their work was. Census information less than 100 years old is not available in order to preserve privacy. The information is available as enumer-ators' returns (already transcribed into readable print) or in the original, hand-written census records. Photocopies of both can be made. Using old maps, pupils can follow the lives of individual families, seeing where they lived, and where they might have worked or spent their leisure hours. Diary entries of one of the people named on the census form can be written,

making reference to other members of the family, with descriptions of the house and surrounding area.

Street or trade directories

These are available in your local history library and list the head of each household and often the profession. Trade directories give extra information about the work which went on.

Account books, sales catalogues, wills and inventories

These are likely to be available only for fairly large houses, and may be time-consuming to get hold of for yourself: ask the owner or at the local history library. Except for the sales catalogues, they can be difficult to read and may require editing and simplification before pupils use them. They give details about the contents of houses; inventories and sales catalogues list the furniture to be found in different rooms, whilst account books and wills may not specify where the objects were kept. If you are visiting a furnished house, groups of pupils can check off the contents of each room against the inventory or catalogue; making a note of anything that is missing, and trying to reason out why – there may not be enough room for all the furniture now that part of the room is roped off for visitors, or the object may have decayed or been broken. In unfurnished houses, allow groups of pupils to take over different rooms, and decide where some of the inventory items would have looked best. Taking one item each, they can sketch this area, and back in school use reference books to find and copy the relevant piece of furniture, which they can cut around and paste onto their sketch.

Archaeological records

These can reveal a wealth of hidden details relating to a ruined house's construction and the materials used, and also add a lot of human detail about what was eaten, or the type of pottery used. They usually contain drawings of finds, but the text tends to be very detailed.

Using census returns and street directories in the school's locality

Houses in the school environs will be lived-in, so all detective work will be based on the exteriors and documentary sources. Firstly find a current large-scale OS map, so that your class can relate the map to what is there now, then start looking at earlier ones, identifying the streets and houses which have survived. The local history librarian will help you in finding a map, street directories and census returns from roughly the same period. If possible, choose two contrasting houses or areas, and get the class to list differences – not just the size, but also proximity of other houses, roads, green spaces, railways, or work places like offices and factories, which will build up a picture of what it was like to actually live there, and how easy it was to get to work. Find out if the houses were south-facing (to catch the sun), or on top of a hill (for the view and clean air). Use the street directory to find the name of the householder, and use this to locate the name on the census (it is easier to use the enumerators' returns, which is a typed copy of the census). Find out about all the household from the census, what their work was, how many there were in the family and if there were servants. It may be possible to work out where people worked or which school the children went to, and what routes they used. When you visit the areas, think about the changes that have happened to the houses and the street, perhaps new windows, doors, a garage, or metalled road surface, street lights, cars. What might have been there instead? What would it have been like to live there? Notes can be taken for writing up later into stories, diary entries, or for use in role play. Drawings of the houses can be made to illustrate the maps or to which can be added the appropriate costumed figures of the family. Your class can research what games were played at the time, what food was eaten, and what work was done. If pairs or small groups work on the individual houses in a street, they can make sketches or silhouettes for a frieze for the classroom wall. Agree a rough scale beforehand. If you use maps or the census covering several dates, you can plot the development of the area and of the families, with illustrated notes on the changes in the houses and the families living in them.

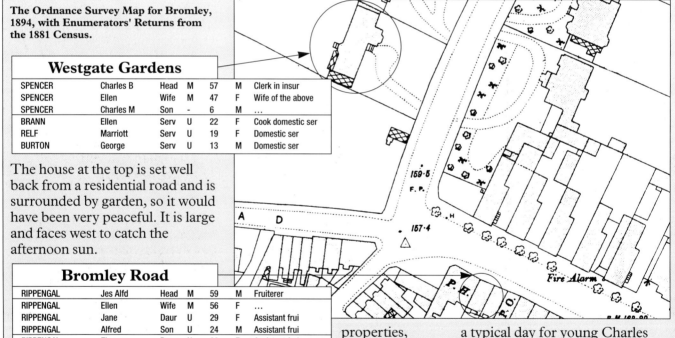

The Ordnance Survey Map for Bromley, 1894, with Enumerators' Returns from the 1881 Census.

Westgate Gardens

SPENCER	Charles B	Head	M	57	M	Clerk in insur
SPENCER	Ellen	Wife	M	47	F	Wife of the above
SPENCER	Charles M	Son	-	6	M	...
BRANN	Ellen	Serv	U	22	F	Cook domestic ser
RELF	Marriott	Serv	U	19	F	Domestic ser
BURTON	George	Serv	U	13	M	Domestic ser

The house at the top is set well back from a residential road and is surrounded by garden, so it would have been very peaceful. It is large and faces west to catch the afternoon sun.

Bromley Road

RIPPENGAL	Jes Alfd	Head	M	59	M	Fruiterer
RIPPENGAL	Ellen	Wife	M	56	F	...
RIPPENGAL	Jane	Daur	U	29	F	Assistant frui
RIPPENGAL	Alfred	Son	U	24	M	Assistant frui
RIPPENGAL	Eleanor	Daur	U	22	F	Assistant frui
RIPPENGAL	Walter	Son	U	21	M	Fruiterers ast
RIPPENGAL	Alice	Daur	U	19	F	Fruiterers ast
RIPPENGAL	Willie	Son	U	16	M	Fruiterers ast
RIPPENGAL	Lewis	Son	U	13	M	Fruiterers ast

The house lower down opens directly onto a busy main street, which was probably noisy and dusty, and is next door to a pub, so evenings may have been rowdy, too. It has an enclosed backyard and is surrounded by similar properties, with no nearby public green space. It is a terraced house, so has windows at the front and back only, and it faces north so it would have been very dark in the front rooms.

Looking at the census returns can stimulate questions about the lifestyles of the two families. For example, how different was a typical day for young Charles Spencer, in his big house, attended by servants and with older than average parents, to that of the full-to-bursting Rippengal household? What clothes, food, furniture, entertainment, washing arrangements might each family have had? What work did Ellen and Harriet do and did they get on? What might Charles Spencer and Lewis Rippengal have thought if they visited each other's homes?

USING HOUSES AND HOMES ACROSS THE CURRICULUM

Houses can be used in a variety of ways to teach specific subjects. The ideas below can be adapted to suit different needs and age ranges. These activities are intended to develop both pupils' knowledge and skills in curriculum areas other than history, and to show how other subjects can be used to solve historical problems and to enhance understanding of the site.

MATHEMATICS

Pupils can use a site investigation to develop their mathematical skills such as measuring, estimating and calculating, and to understand the role maths plays in the design and construction of a house.

The ideal aesthetic proportions for houses with rectangular facades was one where the two different sides bear the relationship of 1:1683, known as the Golden Rectangle. It is reputed to be one of the most satisfying of geometric forms and it was often used horizontally and vertically in Greek and Roman architecture. Later styles based on the classical ones continued to use it.

Your class can draw Golden Rectangles on card, and cut them out so that a Golden Rectangle window is created through which the dimensions of houses can be checked.

By taking measurements of a site pupils can calculate the floor and cubic areas of rooms. This can then be compared with the size of their own living spaces.

Many large houses in the past were designed to keep owners and servants separate and to control access to various areas of the house. Using a plan of the site, different routes around the various rooms can be plotted and compared. This will help pupils to see how people

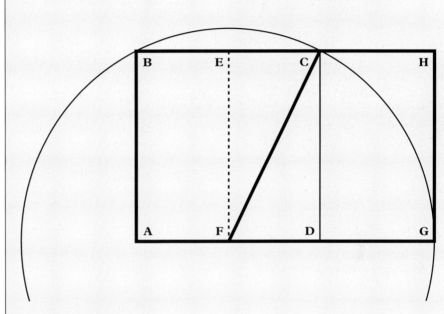

Golden Rectangle
To create your own, make a square, ABCD and mark a mid point on the baseline AD at F. Extend AD and intersect it at G with an arc, using F as the centre point and FC as the radius.

Extend BC and draw a line up at 90° from G to intersect it at H. ABHG is a golden rectangle.

moved around in the house and how this affected their lives and their activities. They can translate their routes into written directions, using measurements calculated from the scale of the plan, and mathematical language, like diagonal, right angle, or obtuse angle. Other members of the class can test the accuracy of these by following them on the plan, or on site.

SCIENCE

Pupils could look at what materials have been used in the construction of the house and why, and they can examine how these have stood the test of time. There may be signs of weathering or erosion caused by atmospheric pollution. They can

think about how the decay could be arrested, and if or how repairs should be carried out.

Many old houses have large grounds which can be used to study plants and wildlife. Comparisons can be made between different parts of the site. Pupils can consider how such factors as climate, soil and the care of the grounds affect the plant and wildlife, and assess the impact of changes to the natural environment.

Forces play an important part in the construction of any house. Pupils can look to see how individual houses manage the forces that act on them. For example, timber-framed houses can direct the force from the weight of the roof inwards

A house with the upper floor slightly larger than the one beneath, giving rise to an overhang, called a jetty.

through heavy beams to a smaller ground floor area. The resultant overhang is called a jetty. In dealing with the same force, the houses in the Rows area of Great Yarmouth are held together with braces, which go all the way through the building, anchoring one side to the other.

The forces used in building work can also be considered, like the use of pulleys, levers, balances and weights.

ENGLISH

Any work on site, particularly when tasks are done in groups, requires pupils to use a range of skills, like listening, asking questions and discussing; reading informational material; and editing and presenting the notes collected on site.

The site can be a stimulus for story-telling. Pupils can develop and perform stories relating to the house, its inhabitants and any historic events associated with it. Encourage them to imagine what it might have been like to live there, sorting out what they can see, smell and hear now and what they might have seen, heard or smelt in the past.

Writing for specific audiences or to a specific brief, like a guide book for very young children, or a TV

script for a documentary on the house, allows children to practice different writing styles and techniques.

TECHNOLOGY

Technology is concerned with exploring ways of meeting people's needs, and this is very much part of the construction and design of a house.

The site can be studied closely in order to identify what the original design brief may have been for the designers and builders. What were the needs of the inhabitants? How were these needs met by the design and construction of the house? Many of the houses that pupils visit are now tourist attractions, and the building has had to change to meet the needs of the visitors, with the addition of lavatories, shop and cafe. Pupils could assess how well this has been done. This will involve them in: identifying the possible audiences which might visit the site, such as school groups, disabled visitors, families, overseas tourists; considering their needs; thinking about how needs differ; and looking at how successfully

Four hundred years ago people cooked their meat by putting rods through it and roasting it in front of the fire.

the site meets these needs at the moment. This can lead to ideas for improvements to the facilities for at least one of these groups.

A variety of equipment can be used to record findings from a visit. Pupils can also explore the ways in which IT can be used to improve the interpretation of the site for a variety of audiences, like young children, or visually impaired visitors.

There are lots of opportunities for useful follow-up research, such as the way in which houses are heated today, how water is collected and piped to houses and rooms within the house, or how bricks are made. Can they apply any of this to their own homes: like finding out where the stopcock is, or the overflow pipe?

GEOGRAPHY

Finding out why a house has been built in a particular place means studying the topographical and geographical features of the area. Aerial photographs and Ordnance Survey maps of the surrounding area will need to be consulted. The impact of the climate and surroundings on the site in both the past and the present can be considered. For vernacular buildings maps can be studied for signs of quarries, and limepits (lime was used to make mortar), or for names like Brick Bank or Quarry Road. Otherwise the transport routes for the materials can be sought by looking for rail, road and canal systems. If you want to extend this type of investigation,

150 years ago people had cookers made of iron. The cookers had ovens, hot water tanks and places on the top to put saucepans.

include searching for the origins of articles in the house, like China vases, Persian carpets, trinkets made in Hong Kong, and so on.

ART

Most houses were designed to be attractive as well as functional, and can be used both as a source of information and as a stimulus to creative work. They display

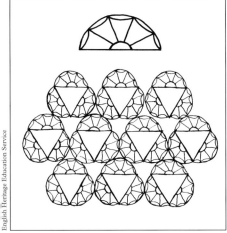

Fanlights designs can be used to create patterns.

A study of door fittings can show a whole range of functional and decorative design.

examples of contemporary design in their fittings and furniture, and exhibit it in their architecture. In addition, historic houses may contain art and sculpture which can be viewed at close quarters.

Pupils can record examples of art, craft and design and use these to help them create their own work based on the decoration, design and construction of the house. For example, they can draw up new designs for a feature of which the original has been replaced, like a door, a light fitting or a staircase, or plan furniture which is modern but which reflects the spirit of a room. Accuracy in recording details like fanlights can be pushed to the limit.

A visit to the site can be used to collect details for work to be done back at school: poster work, ceramics, textiles, collage and printing. There could be constraints to what they produce: for example, they might work on a cheap and cheerful souvenir to be sold on site, or a wallpaper design, or a design for a T shirt.

They can study the evidence at the site and discuss the different craftspeople who would have worked there through the ages and the different techniques that were used. If a site covers a long period of history the different styles can be compared and contrasted.

RELIGIOUS STUDIES

Great medieval and large houses had their own chapels, which were attended by the household every Sunday, and in some houses every day. The owners often selected their own priests or vicars, so to servants it might have seemed on the one hand that they were truly owned, body and soul, or on the other that they belonged to a large, happy family. This can be used to introduce the topic of the part which going to church, chapel, mosque or temple plays in the lives of our communities now.

Roman villas often had a corner as a shrine to the household gods, and the Victorians, in particular, were fond of embroidered texts from the Bible decorating their rooms. Looking at how far religion is an overt part of our lives could be another way into opening a discussion on attitudes in different faiths.

CROSS CURRICULAR THEMES

When studying homes and houses many issues will be raised which may touch on sensitive and controversial topics. In particular you need to be aware of the preconceptions and prejudices that may be faced when looking at issues such as homelessness. The following themes can be used to promote discussion with older pupils.

Education for economic and industrial understanding

Housing touches all our lives. The processes of finding a place to live, and finding ways of paying the rent and mortgage, as well as the upkeep of the property will be faced at some stage by most, if not all pupils. To help them understand the economics, finance and politics of housing, raise some of the following points:

■ who builds houses and why?

■ why do people want to own their own homes?

■ why do they rent rather than buy a house?

■ how do people buy a house?

■ what happens to those people who can't afford a home?

Education for citizenship

Housing requires people to make decisions. Pupils need to be informed about the different choices open to people and about the range of attitudes to these. This can help to develop an understanding of the different ways people choose, or are forced, to live their lives within society. Consider the following areas:

■ different forms of ownership. For example, housing associations, council housing, co-operatives

■ sheltered housing

■ housing provision for people with disabilities

■ different lifestyles across communities

■ homelessness – the causes and solutions; the different types of homelessness such as sleeping rough, living in bed and breakfast accommodation

■ social housing – the role of local and national government in providing housing.

Careers education and guidance

A study of the educational and training choices open to pupils within the housing world may form a part of a career programme. There is a wide range of areas of employment within housing,

English Heritage Photo Library

The chapel at Audley End House, Essex.

including a variety of jobs concerned with the construction and design of houses. There are also those involved in finding people homes, like estate agents, housing managers and others within local government.

Environmental education

Through studying the planning and economic decisions that are made in housing pupils can develop their knowledge and understanding of the ways in which their environment is shaped. This will enable them to identify opportunities for protecting the environment. Issues to think about are:

■ urban planning

■ conservation versus progress – is there a conflict between the preservation of the historic environment and the needs of modern society?

■ environmental housing – recycling, energy conservation, different sources of materials and energy.

Health education

The pupils' own homes are the environment in which they spend much of their time. They need to be aware of the health issues that affect their everyday lives, such as:

■ how to ensure a safe home environment by thinking about how to prevent accidents

■ how houses are designed to meet certain standards of hygiene through sanitation

■ health and personal hygiene in the home

■ public health regulations and housing, in particular the changes in public health laws during the nineteenth and twentieth centuries.

BIBLIOGRAPHY AND RESOURCES

BIBLIOGRAPHY

Reference

Barley, M W, *Houses and History,* 1986, Faber ISBN 0-571-13631-1.

Breckon, B, and Parker, J, *Tracing the History of Houses,* Countryside Books, 1991. ISBN 1-55306-128-X.

Brunskill, R W, *Illustrated Handbook of Vernacular Architecture,* Faber, 1986. ISBN 0-571-13916-7. The standard book on looking at vernacular houses. Well illustrated.

Girouard, M, *Life in the English Country House,* Penguin, 1980. ISBN 0-14-00-5406-5.

Heinemann Ltd, 1976. ISBN 434-95961-8.

Muthesius, S, *The English Terraced House,* Yale, 1982. ISBN 0-3000-02871-7.

Quiney, A, *The Traditional Buildings of England,* Thames and Hudson, 1990. ISBN 0-500-27661-7.

Quiney, A, *Wall to Wall,* BBC Developments, 1994. Booklet to accompany BBC series. ISBN 1-860000-013-4.

Ried, M L, *Prehistoric Houses in Britain,* Shire, 1993. ISBN 0-7478-0218-1.

Many houses have a variety of different textures and patterns.

Gray, E, *The British House: A Concise Architectural History,* Barrie and Jenkins, 1994, ISBN 0-7126-6589-6.

Iredale, D, *Discovering Your Old House,* Shire, 1991. ISBN 0-747800143-6.

N Prizeman, J, *Your House: The Outside View,* Heinemann and Co, 1975. ISBN 0-09-122380-6. Full of excellent pictures of vernacular houses, and different materials.

Ridley, A, *At Home,* William

Pupils

Barden, H, *Houses and Homes,* Wayland, 1994. ISBN 0-7502-0331-5.

Cox, K, and Hughes, P, *History from Photographs: Houses and Homes,* Wayland, 1995. ISBN 0-7502-2123-2.

Chrisp, P, *Living in History: A Tudor Kitchen,* Heinemann, 1997. ISBN 0431-06832-2.

Chrisp, P *Living in History: A Victorian Kitchen,* Heinemann,

1997. ISBN 0431-0682- 6.

Faulkner, L, *A Victorian Kitchen,* Wayland, 1992. ISBN 07502-1159-8.

Finding Out About Homes and Houses Long Ago, Usborne, 1990 ISBN 0-7460-0450-8.

Foster, J, *Homes: A Century of Change, The Twentieth Century,* Hodder and Stoughton, 1990. ISBN 0-340-49941-9.

Gee, A, *Looking at Houses,* Batsford, 1983. ISBN 0-7134-0845-6.

Hamilton-Maclaren, A, *Exploring Technology: Houses and Homes,* Wayland, 1991. ISBN 0-7502-211-4.

Hodgson, P, *Home Life,* Batsford, 1982. ISBN 0-7134-4085-6.

MacDonald, F, *Timelines: Houses,* Franklin Watts, 1994. ISBN 0-7496-1538-9.

Ross, S. *Starting History: Where We Lived,* Wayland, 1994, ISBN 0-7502-1152-0.

Wood, R, *Kitchens Through the Ages,* Wayland, 1997. ISBN 0-7502-2133-X.

Wood, R, *Loos Through the Ages,* Wayland, 1997. ISBN 0-75022134-8.

The *Into the Past* series by Longman deals with houses. Particularly useful for houses from 1900, 1930 and 1950.

The *What Happened Here?* series by A C Black has useful books on houses, including a Tudor farmhouse and a house during the Blitz.

Teaching resources

Keen, J, *Ancient Technology,* English Heritage, 1996. ISBN 1-85074-448-3

Davies, I, and Webb, C, *Using Documents,* English Heritage, 1996 ISBN1-85074- 478-5

Copeland, T, *Geography and the Historic Environment,* English Heritage, 1993.

ISBN 1-85074-332-0

Pownall J, and Hutson, N, *Science and the Historic Environment,* English Heritage, 1992, ISBN 1-85074-381-2

Durbin, G, Morris, S, and Wilkinson, S, *Learning From Objects,* English Heritage, ISBN 1-85074-259-6

Copeland, T, *Maths and the Historic Environment,* English Heritage, 1992 ISBN 1-85074-329-0

Durbin, G, *Using Historic Houses,* English Heritage, 1993. ISBN 1-85074-390-8

Posters
A Roman Villa Fading from View, English Heritage, 1995. A1 size, 1995. For Key Stage 2

Videos
History at Home, English Heritage, 1994, 23 mins. Aimed at parents who want to encourage their children to look at the history in their homes and immediate environment.

The Archaeological Detectives, English Heritage, 1991, 79 mins. Suitable for Key Stage 2. *Clues Challenge,* one of four programmes, looks at finding out about houses.

Paws on the Past, English Heritage, 1996. 20 mins. Suitable for Key Stage 1. Looks at domestic life 100 years ago.

The Milk Jug Mystery, English Heritage, 1997, 20 mins. Suitable for Key Stage 1. Explores a 1940s prefab home.

RESOURCES
If the house you are visiting is formally open to the public, there will most probably be a guide book which will be your starting point. It is worthwhile contacting the manager to find if there are other documents or pictures which will be useful.

Local Studies Library
This is the most likely source for secondary sources relating to the house or houses you are studying. The telephone number will be available from the lending library.

The County Record Office
Primary documentary sources will be housed in the County Record Office. Contact the archivist for information and to book a visit.

Local museum
If you are looking at a house which is an archaeological site, or if the house is a ruin, then the finds or other objects, like furniture and even fittings, will probably be in the local museum. There may also be documents or pictures related to the house.

Archaeology Unit
This may be part of the county or city council. It will have a record of excavations of old houses, and finds from houses of all periods. An archaeologist may be able to come and talk to your class.

Useful contacts
English Heritage cares for many houses which are open to the public. For free gazetteer please see the box at the end of this section. Other useful contacts are:

National Trust
Membership Department
PO Box 39
Bromley BR1 3XL
Tel: 0181 315 1111
Cares for a variety of houses, mainly furnished.

Georgian Group
37 Spital Square
London E1 6DY
Tel: 0171 377 1722
Produces publications and leaflets on Georgian buildings.

Our Education Service aims to help teachers at all levels make best use of the resource of the historic environment. Educational groups can make free visits to over 400 historic properties in the care of English Heritage. The following booklets are free on request. **Visiting Historic Sites** contains a full list of all our sites, details of how to book a visit, and activities for National Curriculum work on site. Our magazine, **Heritage Learning,** is published three times a year. **Resources,** our catalogue, lists all our educational books, videos, posters and slide packs. Please contact:

**English Heritage
Education Service
FREEPOST (WD214)
London SW1E 5YY
Tel: 0171 973 3442
Fax: 0171 973 3443
http://www.
english-heritage.org.uk**

Victorian Society
1 Priory Gardens
London W4 1TT
Tel: 0181 994 1019
Produces useful publications.

Twentieth Century Society
58 Crescent Lane
London SW4 9PU

**Inside back cover:
Gas light, late nineteenth-century**

Pargetting on the Ancient House, Ipswich

Liz Hollinshead